OWNER AND SUBJECT

OWNER NAME _____

MW00953422

_____

HOME PHONE _____

WORK PHONE _____

CELL / MOBILE _____

E-MAIL _____

ADDRESS _____

_____

_____

SUBJECT / TITLE _____

_____

CLASS _____

INSTRUCTOR _____

START DATE _____

END DATE _____

VOLUME _____

NOTES _____

_____

Please contact the owner if you find this notebook. Thank you.

Hexagonal Graph Paper Notebook
2 Inch (2") Hexagons - 1 Inch (1") Radius - Horizontally Aligned Grid
8.5" x 11" - 21.59 cm x 27.94 cm
200 Pages - 100 Sheets - White Paper - Page Numbers
Table of Contents - Owner / Subject Page
Softcover - Perfect Bound

We have a wide assortment of notebooks, journals, diaries, manuscript paper, calendars, planners, log books and other products.   Choose from an extensive selection of cover designs, page sizes, page counts, paper, formats, styles and languages.

www.CactusPublishing.com

Sample Page
Hexagonal Graph Paper
2 Inch (2") Hexagons
1 Inch (1") Radius
Horizontally Aligned Grid

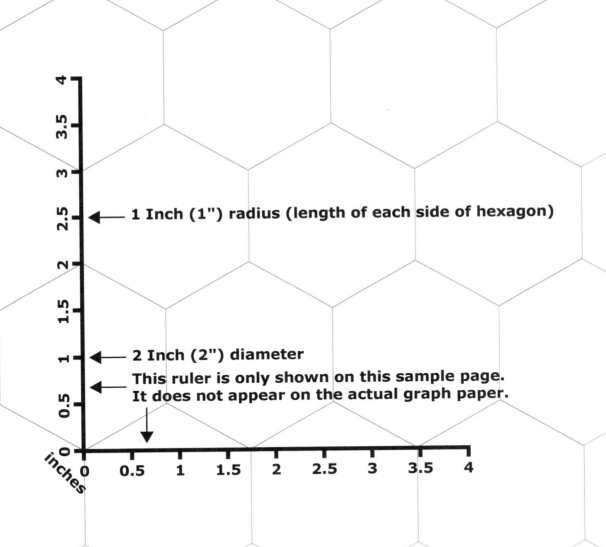

← 1 Inch (1") radius (length of each side of hexagon)

← 2 Inch (2") diameter

← This ruler is only shown on this sample page.
It does not appear on the actual graph paper.

This sample page shows the page number as iii.
The notebook pages are numbered from 1 to 200
and start after the table of contents.

IMPORTANT NOTES

TABLE OF CONTENTS

DATE	DESCRIPTION / TOPIC / SUBJECT	PAGE

TABLE OF CONTENTS

DATE	DESCRIPTION / TOPIC / SUBJECT	PAGE

TABLE OF CONTENTS

DATE	DESCRIPTION / TOPIC / SUBJECT	PAGE

TABLE OF CONTENTS

DATE	DESCRIPTION / TOPIC / SUBJECT	PAGE

TABLE OF CONTENTS

DATE	DESCRIPTION / TOPIC / SUBJECT	PAGE

TABLE OF CONTENTS

DATE	DESCRIPTION / TOPIC / SUBJECT	PAGE

TOC-6

TABLE OF CONTENTS

DATE	DESCRIPTION / TOPIC / SUBJECT	PAGE

TABLE OF CONTENTS

DATE	DESCRIPTION / TOPIC / SUBJECT	PAGE

TOC-8

5

8

9

16

19

23

34

39

43

50

51

54

62

63

73

74

88

89

122

124

128

129

133

140

143

144

148

149

159

174

180

181

189

192

194

195

199

Made in United States
Troutdale, OR
01/04/2024